DATE DUE

1986 Production Printing, School District No. 11
Standard Form No. 88160
1000/Pkg.

CONTEMPORARY AMERICAN
SUCCESS STORIES

Famous People of Hispanic Heritage
Volume IV

Barbara J. Marvis

A Mitchell Lane
Multicultural Biography Series
• Celebrating Diversity •

CONTEMPORARY AMERICAN SUCCESS STORIES
Famous People of Hispanic Heritage

VOLUME I
Geraldo Rivera
Melissa Gonzalez
Federico Peña
Ellen Ochoa

VOLUME II
Tommy Nuñez
Margarita Esquiroz
Cesar Chavez
Antonia Novello

VOLUME III
Giselle Fernandez
Jon Secada
Desi Arnaz
Joan Baez

VOLUME IV
Selena Quintanilla Pérez
Robert Rodriguez
Josefina López
Alfredo Estrada

VOLUME V
Gloria Estefan
Fernando Cuza
Rosie Perez
Cheech Marin

VOLUME VI
Pedro José Greer
Nancy Lopez
Rafael Palmeiro
Hilda Perera

VOLUME VII
Raul Julia
Mariah Carey
Andres Galarraga
Mary Joe Fernandez

VOLUME VIII
Cristina Saralegui
Trent Dimas
Nydia Velázquez
Jimmy Smits

VOLUME IX
Roy Benavidez
Isabel Allende
Oscar De La Hoya
Jackie Guerra

VOLUME X
Rebecca Lobo
Carlos Mencia
Linda Chavez Thom
Bill Richardson

Publisher's Cataloging in Publication
Marvis, Barbara J.
    Famous people of Hispanic heritage. Vol. IV / Barbara J. Marvis

      p. cm. —(Contemporary American success stories)—(A Mitchell Lane multicultural biography series)
    Includes index.
    LCCN: 95-75963
    ISBN: 1-883845-30-0 (hc)
    ISBN: 1-883845-29-7 (pbk)

      1. Hispanic Americans—Biography—Juvenile literature. I. Title.
II. Series.

E184.S75M37 1996

920'.009268
QBI96-20404

Illustrated by Barbara Tidman
Project Editor: Susan R. Scarfe

Mitchell Lane PUBLISHERS

Your Path To Quality Educational Material
P. O. Box 200
Childs, Maryland 21916-0200

TABLE OF CONTENTS

Acknowledgments

Every reasonable effort has been made to gain copyright permission where such permission has been deemed necessary. Any oversight brought to the publisher's attention will be corrected in future printings.

Most of the stories in this series were written through personal interviews and/or with the complete permission of the person, representative of the person, or family of the person being profiled, and are authorized biographies. Though we attempted to contact personally each and every person profiled within, for various reasons we were unable to authorize every story. All stories have been thoroughly researched and checked for accuracy, and to the best of our knowledge represent true stories.

We wish to acknowledge with gratitude the generous help of Elaine DagenBela and MaryRose Walls of the Hispanic Heritage Awards for their recommendations of those we have profiled in this series. Our greatest appreciation also goes to Katherine Moore and Mark Thornhill for their help with our story of Robert Rodriguez, and Elizabeth Avellan (telephone interview April 11, 1996) and Robert Rodriguez (telephone interview May 24, 1996) for their time and help with the story of and photographs of Robert Rodriguez; Josefina López (telephone interview March 10, 1996) and Jon Mercedes for their information, patience, considerable time, and photographs of Josefina López; Alfredo Estrada (telephone interview March 5, 1996) and Barbara Fernandez for our story about and photographs of Alfredo Estrada; and Joe Villarreal and Sandy Friedman for help with our story about Selena Quintanilla Pérez.

Photograph Credits

The quality of the photographs in this book may vary; many of them are personal snapshots supplied to us courtesy of the person being profiled. Many are very old, one-of-a-kind photos. Most are not professional photographs, nor were they intended to be. The publisher felt that the personal nature of the stories in this book would only be enhanced by real-life, family album–type photos, and chose to include many interesting snapshots, even if they were not quite the best quality. p.15 courtesy EMI Records; p.23 AP/Wide World Photos; p.24, p.26 Reuters/Archive Photos; p.28 AP/Wide World Photos; p.33, p.34, p.35, p.37, p.39, p.43, p.45, p.51, p.55 courtesy Rebecca and Cecilio Rodriguez; p.57 courtesy Miramax Films; p.58, p.60 courtesy Rebecca and Cecilio Rodriguez; p.65, p.66, p.67, p.68, p.69, p.70, p.73, p.75, p.77, p.79, p.81, p.82, p.84, p.85 courtesy Josefina López; p.89, p.93 (bottom) courtesy Alfredo Estrada; p.93 (top) Barbara Marvis; p.95 courtesy Alfredo Estrada.

About the Author

Barbara Marvis has been a professional writer for twenty years. Motivated by her own experience with ethnic discrimination as a young Jewish girl growing up in suburban Philadelphia, Ms. Marvis developed the **Contemporary American Success Stories** series to dispel racial and ethnic prejudice, to tell culturally diverse stories that maintain ethnic and racial distinction, and to provide positive role models for young minorities. She is the author of several books for young adults, including **Tommy Nuñez: NBA Referee/Taking My Best Shot**. She holds a B.S. degree in English and communications from West Chester State University and an M.Ed in remedial reading from the University of Delaware.

INTRODUCTION

by Kathy Escamilla

One of the fastest growing ethno-linguistic groups in the United States is a group of people who are collectively called Hispanic. The term *Hispanic* is an umbrella term that encompasses people from many nationalities, from all races, and from many social and cultural groups. The label *Hispanic* sometimes obscures the diversity of people who come from different countries and speak different varieties of Spanish. Therefore, it is crucial to know that the term *Hispanic* encompasses persons whose origins are from Spanish-speaking countries, including Spain, Mexico, Central and South America, Cuba, Puerto Rico, the Dominican Republic, and the United States. It is important also to note that Spanish is the heritage language of most Hispanics. However, Hispanics living in the United States are also linguistically diverse. Some speak mostly Spanish and little English, others are bilingual, and some speak only English.

Hispanics are often also collectively called Latinos. In addition to calling themselves Hispanics or Latinos, many people in this group also identify themselves in more specific terms according to their country of origin or their ethnic group (e.g., Cuban-American, Chicano, Puerto Rican-American, etc.). The population of Hispanics in the United States is expected to triple in the next twenty-five years, making it imperative that students in schools understand and appreciate the enormous contributions that persons of Hispanic heritage have made in the Western Hemisphere in general and in the United States in particular.

There are many who believe that in order to be successful in the United States now and in the twenty-first century, all persons from diverse cultural backgrounds, such as Hispanics, should be assimilated. To be assimilated means losing one's distinct cultural and linguistic heritage and changing to or adopting the cultural attributes of the dominant culture.

Others disagree with the assimilationist viewpoint and believe that it is both possible and desirable for persons from diverse cultural backgrounds to maintain their cultural heritage and also to contribute positively and successfully to the dominant culture. This viewpoint is called cultural pluralism, and it is from the perspective of cultural pluralism that these biographies are written. They represent persons who identify strongly with their Hispanic heritage and at the same time who are proud of being citizens of the United States and successful contributors to U.S. society.

The biographies in these books represent the diversity of Hispanic heritage in the United States. Persons featured are contemporary figures whose national origins range from Argentina to Arizona and whose careers and contributions cover many aspects of contemporary life in the United States. These biographies include writers, musicians, actors, journalists, astronauts, businesspeople, judges, political activists, and politicians. Further, they include Hispanic women and men, and thus also characterize the changing role of all women in the United States. Each person profiled in this book is a positive role model, not only for persons of Hispanic heritage, but for any person.

Collectively, these biographies demonstrate the value of cultural pluralism and a view that the future strength of the United States lies in nurturing the diversity of its human potential, not in its uniformity.

Dr. Kathy Escamilla is currently Vice President of the National Association for Bilingual Education and an Associate Professor of Bilingual Education and Multicultural Education at the University of Colorado, Denver. She previously taught at the University of Arizona, and was the Director of Bilingual Education for the Tucson Unified School District in Tucson, Arizona. Dr. Escamilla earned a B.A. degree in Spanish and Literature from the University of Colorado in 1971. Her master's degree is in bilingual education from the University of Kansas, and she earned her doctorate in bilingual education from UCLA in 1987.

MAP OF THE WORLD

SELENA QUINTANILLA PÉREZ

Tejano Singer
1971-1995

"You can sing with the angels, now."

Graffiti from a fan after the singer's death, April 1995

BIO HIGHLIGHTS

- Born April 16, 1971, in Lake Jackson, Texas; mother: Marcela; father: Abraham Quintanilla
- Moved to Corpus Christi, Texas, after her father's restaurant failed
- 1981, at the age of nine, began singing with the family band
- Learned to sing in Spanish from her father
- Left school after eighth grade to travel with the family band. Earned her GED through home school courses
- 1985, made her first commercial recording
- 1987, won the Tejano Music Awards in San Antonio for best female vocalist and performer of the year
- 1989, signed with EMI Latin to record Spanish-language music
- 1991, gave Yolanda Saldívar the unpaid position of founding her fan club
- Married Chris Pérez, the band's guitarist, on April 2, 1992
- 1994, received Grammy for *Selena Live!*
- 1994, received an English-language contract from SBK records
- August 1994, Selena put Yolanda in charge of her new business, Selena Etc., Inc.
- January to March 1995, the Quintanillas heard rumors that Yolanda was taking money from the business
- March 30, 1995, Selena tried to discuss financial discrepancies with Yolanda
- March 31, 1995, Selena was shot by Yolanda Saldívar at the Days Inn in Corpus Christi. She died at 1:05 P.M. at Memorial Medical Center
- EMI released *Dreaming of You*, an album that Selena was making at the time of her death
- Three days after she was shot, the movie *Don Juan DeMarco*, in which Selena had a small acting part, premiered

The Quintanilla family has lived and worked in Texas for at least a hundred years.

▲▲▲▲▲▲

SELENA QUINTANILLA PÉREZ

On March 30, 1995, Marcela Quintanilla received a phone call from her daughter, Selena. "Mom," she said, "let's go have lunch."

"My foot was swollen," remembers Mrs. Quintanilla. "I'd broken my ankle, but I wanted to spend the time with her. I'm so glad I went. We sat in this restaurant for about four hours, and she told me about another time she'd eaten there. A little old lady was eating by herself. Selena felt bad for her so she told the waiter she wanted to pay for the lady's meal, but not to say who did it. Later, Selena called the waiter over and said, 'I want you to give her one of those little cakes you give people on their birthdays. Put it in a bag so she can take it home.' When she told me this story, I wanted to cry. Then Selena drove me home. She was weaving in and out of traffic and singing. I grabbed her ear and said, 'I love you.' And she said, 'I love you, Mama.' When we got back, she came in and talked to her father for a few minutes. Then she said, 'I've got to get home to my husband—he's waiting for me.' She left. And I didn't see her again."

The very next day, Selena was shot to death by her fan-club president and boutique manager, Yolanda Saldívar, in a dispute over missing funds. The beautiful Tejano singer was just two weeks shy of her twenty-fourth birthday and two days short of her third wedding anniversary to Chris Pérez, her band's guitarist. Her tragic death cut short a career that was on the brink of international success.

Selena Quintanilla was born on April 16, 1971, in Lake Jackson, Texas, a small town seventy-five miles southwest of Houston. She was the youngest of three children born to Marcela and Abraham Quintanilla, Jr. Selena had an older brother, Abraham III (A.B.), who was eight years her senior, and a sister, Suzette, who was four years older than she.

The Quintanilla family has lived and worked in Texas for at least a hundred years. They are of Mexican ancestry. Selena's great grandfather, Eulojio Quintanilla, was born in northern Mexico in 1886 and came to Texas not long after. His wife, Doloris (Selena's great grandmother), was born in the United States in 1892.

Selena spent her early childhood in Lake Jackson, which is one of nine small towns on the flat coastal plains of Brazoria County. Though commercial fishing also supports the town, chemicals are the mainstay of the economy there. Abraham Quintanilla worked for Dow Chemical as a shipping clerk in those early years. But his real passion had always been music. According to his brother, Eddie Quintanilla, Abraham loved street-corner doo-wop music and rhythm and blues, but he played traditional Tex-Mex music—polkas and waltzes with Spanish music—when he was in high school (1950s) with a band he belonged to called *Los Dinos* (The Boys). He was

▼▼▼▼▼

Selena spent her early childhood in Lake Jackson, which is one of nine small towns in Brazoria County.

▲▲▲▲▲▲

They formed a little band they called *Selena y Los Dinos* after Abraham's high-school band.

Selena Quintanilla Pérez

the vocalist. Abraham recognized Selena's musical talents when she was quite young.

One day, when Selena was just five, her father was playing the guitar in their home. Selena came over to his knee and began to sing. Her voice was pure and her pitch was perfect. "I could see it from day one," her father said. "She loved all music." So Abraham soundproofed his garage and began teaching his children about the music he loved so much. They formed a little band they called *Selena y Los Dinos* after Abraham's high-school band. A.B. was on bass, Suzette played drums, and Selena sang. They also included two other children in their band: Rodney Pyeatt and Rena Dearman. Before long, they were playing at weddings and parties.

Selena attended first grade at Oran M. Roberts Elementary School. The students there were from all over Latin America, and also included Anglo-Americans and African-Americans. Many of her classmates were from Chile and Argentina. Their parents had come to Dow Chemical through a special training program.

Selena's first-grade teacher, Nina McGlashan, teaches at the same school today. She remembers Selena very clearly. "She tried really hard at whatever she was doing and was eager to learn—just the kind of student you always like to have. What I remember is that big smile. Selena had a real perky personality. She participated in everything. She was easy to get along with and very well liked by the other children."

Selena Quintanilla Pérez

In 1980, Abraham Quintanilla quit his job at Dow Chemical to start his own Tex-Mex restaurant, which he called Papagallo's. The whole family pitched in to help make it work. All the children had chores at the struggling restaurant. On most weekends, their band performed. But no matter how hard they worked, the restaurant went under only one year later. The area was caught in a recession caused by the Texas oil bust, and people stopped going out to eat. As a result of the restaurant failure, the Quintanillas lost their home, many of their possessions, and, above all, their livelihood. In 1981, when Selena was only nine, the family moved to Corpus Christi, where they started their musical career out of necessity. "We had no alternative," Selena recalled in a 1992 interview.

The family made music their full-time career as they traveled across Texas and the United States in a battered van pulling a broken-down trailer. They mostly toured the back country of South Texas, playing everywhere from wedding halls to honky-tonks. "If we got ten people in one place, that was great," said Selena. "We ate a lot of hamburgers and shared everything."

Selena's father managed the band. He thought they would be most successful going the Tejano route. Tejano is a lively Spanish-language blend of Tex-Mex rhythms, pop-style tunes, and German polka that was not all that popular at the time. The only problem was, Selena didn't speak any Spanish. Selena had been raised to speak

The family made music their full-time career as they traveled across Texas and the United States in a battered van pulling a broken-down trailer.

A lot of
people
knew
Selena
from her
appearances
on *The
Johnny
Canales
Show.*

SELENA QUINTANILLA PÉREZ

only English at home and at school. Her father had to teach her Spanish phonetically; it was through music that Selena learned to speak Spanish.

In Corpus Christi, Selena attended West Oso Junior High School. She was an excellent student, but she was forced to stop going when she was in eighth grade, because she was on the road so much with her family. She did continue her schooling through home school courses and went on to earn her equivalency degree. Selena felt she missed most of her teen years because she could not attend school, and she later became an advocate of all children completing their high-school education. She felt she had many life experiences during her teen years, however, that made her seem far more mature than her years. Selena made her first commercial recording in 1985, for a small Texas label (San Antonio-based Manny Guerra), when she was just fourteen years old.

While the Quintanillas were on the road, they frequently ran into another traveling bandsman at dances, weddings, and other festivals. His name was Johnny Canales. Johnny knew Abraham from their days in high school, when they both had bands. Later, Johnny would host his own international Spanish-language television program, *The Johnny Canales Show.* When Selena was twelve or thirteen, she first performed on Johnny's show, and she appeared about a dozen more times over the years.

SELENA QUINTANILLA PÉREZ

"When she was young and starting out, our show was small, about five TV stations," Johnny remembers. "Over the years, as [Selena] grew, we did, too. It's like we've grown up together." A lot of people knew Selena from her appearances on *The Johnny Canales Show.* She became an instant hit just as the show was beginning to be a big hit as well. Today, *The Johnny Canales Show* is broadcast internationally on the Univision network, bringing Tejano music into twenty-three countries, over five hundred stations, in nearly two hundred markets.

Johnny Canales remembers when he first realized that Selena was headed for stardom. "We took her across the border to Matamoros in 1986, and I was dying to see how the Mexican people would react. She took the stage and they went wild."

Selena was part of the Tejano culture. Tejano music was in her blood.

▼▼▼▼▼

Selena's lifelong ambition was to take her music across all racial, cultural, and economic barriers.

▲▲▲▲▲▲

But even as recently as 1988, the family didn't make very much money. "In 1988, the family was playing in Idaho, and they were staying in a small hotel because money was still tight," Johnny recalls. "The Quintanillas had just purchased an old over-the-road coach. There were seats in the front and mattresses laid out in back. At the end of their show, Selena was sitting in the front seat eating a late dinner of potted meat and weenies. I said, 'Selena, are you still eating that stuff?' and she said, 'Yes, I don't want to get used to the good life.'"

When *Selena y Los Dinos* was just starting out, Tejano music was not very popular in Mexico. It was nearly forbidden in Puerto Rico and the Puerto Rican neighborhoods of New York City. It was shunned in Florida. That is, until they heard Selena.

Selena's lifelong ambition was to take her music across all racial, cultural, and economic barriers. This was not an easy task. Selena was part of the Tejano culture. The Tejano music was in her blood. The Tejanos were originally Mexican-Americans who were born or lived in Texas. They experienced a difficult type of prejudice that many other Latino groups in America did not even know existed. The Anglo-Texans often discriminated against them, and though it is not a constant problem today, there are still open incidents of ethnic bias. The Mexicans (on the other side of the border) often held many prejudices against the Tejanos as well. Most young

Tejanos speak and read only English, and, according to the Mexicans, none of the Tejanos speaks Spanish correctly. The Tejanos even refer to their language as "Spanglish." Selena wanted her music to moderate the ethnic prejudice many in Texas felt.

As the band received increasing recognition, Selena's father continued to do all he could to support his rising star. He managed the band, handled the bookings, worked the sound boards, and collected the money. In 1987, Selena won the Tejano Music Awards in San Antonio for female vocalist and performer of the year. This was a big break for the Quintanillas, who had graduated to singing in ballrooms and cut nearly a dozen albums for their regional label. In 1989, Abraham signed a breakthrough six-figure deal for the band to cut Spanish-language records for EMI's new Latin division. The old tour coach was replaced with the most modern Silver Eagle coaches: one bus for the Quintanilla family and one for the band. There were six increasingly successful albums, topped by *Selena Live!*, which received a Grammy in 1994 for the best Mexican-American performance, then her last complete album, *Amor Prohibido* (Forbidden Love), which was nominated for a Grammy and sold over 500,000 copies. Selena was a total package: she was smart, she was beautiful, she could sing, and she could move. She was a millionaire by the time she was 19. At 21, she drew a crowd of 20,000 people to the fairgrounds in Pasadena,

▼▼▼▼▼

In 1989, Abraham signed a breakthrough six-figure deal for the band to cut Spanish-language records for EMI's new Latin division.

▲▲▲▲▲▲

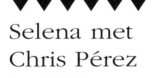

Selena met Chris Pérez in 1988 when she went to San Antonio to attend a rehearsal of his band.

SELENA QUINTANILLA PÉREZ

Texas. In 1994, 60,000 people showed up to hear her sing in Houston. It was not long before she moved to the big time. Later in 1994, the band received an English-language contract from SBK records (a division of EMI), and Selena was set to record her first all-English album that would bring her her dream and cross her over to mainstream America. She was on the road to international stardom. The album was to be released in mid-1995.

Selena met Chris Pérez in 1988 when she went to San Antonio to attend a rehearsal of his band. He was twenty years old at the time, two years older than Selena. Chris joined *Selena y Los Dinos* as a guitarist in 1989, but it was not until 1991 that their romance began. For two years, they toured together as friends. Then one day, Selena's brother, A.B., hinted to Chris that Selena might be interested in being more than just friends. According to Chris, when he got the message, he realized his feelings were more than just friendship as well. They were in the Pizza Hut in Rio Grande Valley when Chris finally admitted to Selena that he would like their relationship to be something more. "I never wanted to see anyone else, I never went out with anyone else," Chris says. "It was just Selena and me." Selena told Chris she felt the same way and, little by little, it all came together. Chris and Selena were married on April 2, 1992. Friends and neighbors say they made a cute couple. Chris wore a short ponytail, which they found acceptable for a musician, and they saw him as an attentive, doting husband. The two were always holding hands.

Though her career advanced rapidly in the 1990s, she and her family never left the modest Molina neighborhood of Corpus Christi where she was raised. Selena built three homes right next to each other. She and her husband lived in one house; her mother and father lived in the middle house; and A.B. and his wife, Vangie, lived on the other side. Except for the expensive Silver Eagle coaches, the only other sign of wealth in the neighborhood was the Porsche automobile that Selena drove. In 1995, Selena and Chris were designing a 10-bedroom home on 10 acres of land in town so that the couple could have some privacy. It was to be Selena's dream home.

Selena continued to become more and more popular. Fame and fortune did nothing, however, to change the little girl from Corpus Christi. Selena's personality did not change as she grew more famous. She still wanted to remember the people who had supported her singing all those years. "Everybody loved Selena," a neighbor says, "not only because of her beauty and talent, but because of the way she was. Though she was famous, she would act just like any other person. She shopped at Wal-Mart and ate at Pizza Hut." Even Johnny Canales, who knew Selena from the time she was very young, said fame never changed her.

▼▼▼▼▼

"Everybody loved Selena, not only because of her beauty and talent, but because of the way she was. Though she was famous, she would act just like any other person."

▲▲▲▲▲

SELENA QUINTANILLA PÉREZ

Selena's popularity in the music world gave rise to many other business ventures that the Quintanillas had only dreamed about before 1991. Suddenly there were hit records, albums, a Grammy, concert and nightclub appearances, product endorsements, two promising boutiques, and then a fan club.

Selena was seen in public a great deal, but her family tried to maintain her privacy. Her father was very protective, often ushering her through adoring crowds to keep her from getting knocked over. Other men in the family protected Selena when her father was not around. But as her fame grew, so did the number of her fans. She became exceptionally popular, especially in south Texas. Among her fans was a registered nurse from San Antonio. Her name was Yolanda Saldívar.

In early 1991, Yolanda began calling Abraham Quintanilla about forming a fan club for Selena. She left repeated messages for him. At first, Abraham did not return her calls. Eventually the family decided the fan club might be a good idea, and they spoke to Yolanda about it.

Yolanda came from a big family in San Antonio. She was a loner, she was very quiet, she had no friends, she never married, and she had no children. She lived in a modest house with her mother and was a nurse at nearby hospitals. Other than the fact that she was the aunt of one of Selena's childhood friends, no one in Selena's family knew anything about her. But she

In early 1991, Yolanda Saldívar began calling Abraham Quintanilla about forming a fan club for Selena.

was so enthusiastic, and she idolized Selena so, that she soon won Selena's support. In 1991, Selena gave her the unpaid position of founding a fan club. Yolanda became a faithful supporter.

Shortly after Saldívar was hired, Selena raved about her to the press. "She's doing exceptionally well," she said. "Fan clubs can ruin you if people get upset and turned off by them. But she's doing really good." Selena showed her friendship by showering Yolanda with gifts. Yolanda was crazy about cows, and Selena bought her an $800 rug with a cow on it. Then she bought her a cow phone. Yolanda seemed utterly devoted to Selena.

In August 1994, Selena rewarded Yolanda by moving her to a paid position. She put Yolanda in charge of her new business venture, and Yolanda quit her position as a nurse. Selena opened a boutique called Selena Etc., Inc. One shop was opened in Corpus Christi and another in San Antonio. The shops sold a line of fashions and jewelry designed by Selena, and they also had salons for hairstyling and manicures. Selena Etc. was also involved in selling its products to other stores. But it was not long before Yolanda began having problems with the other employees.

Martin Gomez was hired by the family to help produce the fashion lines. The fashions were called Martin Gomez Designs for Selena. "From the beginning," said Gomez, "there was a lot of

▼▼▼▼▼▼

Shortly after Saldívar was hired, Selena raved about her to the press.

▲▲▲▲▲▲

▼▼▼▼▼▼

"I told
Selena I
was afraid
of Yolanda.
She
wouldn't let
me talk to
Selena
anymore."

▲▲▲▲▲▲

tension between Yolanda and me. She was mean and manipulative." In January 1995, Gomez quit out of frustration. "I told Selena I was afraid of Yolanda," he said. "She wouldn't let me talk to Selena anymore. She was too possessive."

Out of loyalty to Yolanda, Selena did nothing. But employees of the boutique and others close to Selena saw a problem arising. Yolanda quickly began to take over Selena's life. Soon she had built a protective shield between Selena and the public.

One day in late 1994, there was an important style show at which some of Selena's new fashions were being introduced. Some friends and customers showed up early at the hotel in Corpus Christi where the show was being held. Before the doors had opened, there was a line waiting to get in. In that line was longtime family friend Rosita Rodela.

Rosita tried to get in to see Selena and Abraham before the show, but Yolanda wouldn't let her. "You can't come in," Yolanda said sharply. "It isn't open yet. You have to get back." She was very rude.

Rosita was shocked because Yolanda's behavior was in such contrast to the warm, courteous nature of the entire Quintanilla family. "I told her I was a friend of the family and I was sure they would see me. I asked to go see Abraham."

"He's busy," Yolanda snapped. But just at that moment, Abraham walked by and saw Rosita. She asked him if they could chat, and he said sure. Yolanda's eyes pierced Rosita as she walked through the door.

For Christmas in 1994, Selena's employees took up a collection to purchase a custom-made ring for her. The ring was a 14-carat gold and diamond ring with a white gold egg, encrusted with fifty-two small diamonds. While all the employees had contributed to buying the ring, it appears that Yolanda led Selena to believe it was a personal gift from her alone. It was later believed that Yolanda in fact pocketed the employees' money and charged the ring to one of Selena's credit cards.

The white-gold egg ring that Selena is wearing was given to her as a Christmas present by her employees.

In late January, Abraham began hearing rumors about problems with the fan club. Several fans complained that they had sent in their $22 membership fee for the fan club but had not received the promised T-shirt, CD, or photograph. About the same time, other employees began to raise questions about Yolanda. They said it appeared that Yolanda had been taking money

Yolanda Saldívar was charged with and convicted of the murder of Selena. She is shown here with her lawyer.

from the business. Some of the employees' paychecks bounced, and there were rumors that Yolanda had bought herself a new truck with company funds. Abraham decided to confront Yolanda about the accusations without telling Selena. Yolanda denied doing anything wrong.

In early March, some employees from the San Antonio boutique revealed to Selena that Yolanda appeared to be taking money from the store. Abraham, Selena, and her sister, Suzette, met with Yolanda and demanded a full accounting. Yolanda claimed there were people who just wanted to make her look bad.

On March 13, after undergoing a background check, Yolanda Saldívar purchased a snub-nosed .38-caliber pistol from a San Antonio gun shop. Then she went to Monterrey, Mexico, where Selena was planning to open another boutique. She took all of Selena's business records with her. At some point during the trip, Selena called Yolanda and told her to bring the records back.

On March 30, Yolanda called Selena to tell her she had brought the financial records back to Corpus Christi. She told her she would discuss the matter with her, if she would come to the Days Inn, where Yolanda was staying. She told her to come alone. Instead, Chris accompanied Selena to the hotel. The two returned home later that day without all the documents. There were still bank statements missing.

On the morning of March 31, Selena left home at 9 A.M. Yolanda had asked her to go with her to Doctor's Regional Medical Center, claiming that she had been raped in Monterrey. When the medical tests came back inconclusive, Yolanda admitted she had made up the story. Selena and Yolanda went back to Room 158 at the Days Inn to get the missing records.

When Selena asked Yolanda for the bank statements, the two exchanged harsh words. Selena decided to end their professional relationship by firing her. Yolanda then demanded that Selena return the ring on her finger, which had been a Christmas gift from her employees. As Selena went to take the ring from her finger, Yolanda pulled out a gun.

A maid at the Days Inn saw Selena run from the room. Yolanda chased her and shot her in the back. The bullet entered her right shoulder

▼▼▼▼▼▼

As Selena went to take the ring from her finger, Yolanda pulled out a gun.

▲▲▲▲▲▲

and severed an artery. Selena stumbled into the motel office asking for help. The desk clerk called 911. The call came just before noon.

Lidia Castaneda, a friend of the family, mourns at Selena's funeral.

An ambulance arrived within three minutes and whisked Selena to Memorial Medical Center. The hospital notified Abraham that his daughter had been in an accident and they must come right away. The family thought she had been in a car wreck. It was not until they arrived at the hospital that they found out she had been shot.

SELENA QUINTANILLA PÉREZ

There was nothing more the doctors could do. Selena bled to death just after 1:00 P.M.

In the meantime, Yolanda Saldívar sat in her truck outside the Days Inn and held the police at bay for nine hours. Finally, she surrendered to police and was taken away to the Nueces County jail.

On April 3, 1995, Selena Quintanilla Pérez was buried in Corpus Christi. More than 30,000 people walked by her casket the day before to pay their last respects. Hundreds of vigils, candlelight marches, and memorial Masses were held for Selena in the days following her death. It was difficult for her family to grieve in such a public way. There were hundreds of news stories, television shows, and magazine articles about Selena. Ironically, she became much more famous in her death.

After Selena died, sales of her last album, *Amor Prohibido*, almost tripled, reaching 1.5 million copies. Business boomed at her Corpus Christi boutique. EMI Records decided to take advantage of the publicity, and they quickly released *Dreaming of You*, an album that Selena was making at the time of her death. The album contains five songs in English that she had recorded for the album. That was all that had been cut. Using the latest technology, EMI was able to lift her Spanish vocals from a song that had been released years earlier and mix them with new vocals by the group Barrio Boyzz. In addition, they included several songs that Selena had

▼▼▼▼▼
After Selena died, sales of her last album, *Amor Prohibido*, almost tripled.
▲▲▲▲▲▲

just recorded for the movie *Don Juan DeMarco*, in which Selena had had a small part with a Mexican mariachi band. In fact, the movie was released just a few days after her death. (Its release date had been planned many months before.)

There is no doubt that Selena was on the brink of international stardom when she was murdered. The fact that her business has flourished after her death is testimony to that.

Selena has millions of fans all around the globe. Many young girls in Texas want to be just like her.

Selena had a cameo role in the movie *Don Juan DeMarco*, a New Line Cinema release that opened nationwide on April 7, 1995.

She was more than a singer; she was also like a big sister. Before her death, Selena visited schools in predominantly Mexican-American neighborhoods all over the United States. She would remind the kids to stay in school, to not use drugs, and to be careful about sex. She told the children it was all right to aspire to be singers, but they must get their education, too. Days after her

death, the Texas legislature unanimously passed a resolution honoring Selena's accomplishments as a role model for the state's youth, including her work educating Latinos about the dangers of drugs and AIDS.

Senator Eddie Lucio (D-Brownsville) said, "We're going to think about her as years go by, and Selena will be eternally young in the hearts and souls of all of us."

"We're going to think about her as years go by, and Selena will be eternally young in the hearts and souls of all of us."

SELECTED DISCOGRAPHY

Ven Conmigo	(Come with Me)	
	1991	EMI Latin
Entre a Mi Mundo	(Come into My World)	
	1992	EMI Latin
Selena Live!	1993	EMI Latin
Amor Prohibido	(Forbidden Love)	
	1994	EMI Latin
Dreaming of You	1995	EMI/ EMI Latin

ROBERT RODRIGUEZ

Film Writer, Director, Producer
1968-

"My advice to aspiring filmmakers is first of all to quit aspiring. If you really want to make movies, just do it to have fun. Don't do it to be famous or because you think you'll make a lot of money. You have to enjoy what you're doing. Don't feel you have to be an overnight success, either. The more you practice, the better you'll be.**"**

Robert Rodriguez, as told to Barbara Marvis, May 1996

BIO HIGHLIGHTS

- Born June 20, 1968, in San Antonio, Texas; mother: Rebecca Villegas; father: Cecilio Rodriguez
- Began making short videos when he was in junior high school
- Met Carlos Gallardo in high school
- Attended University of Texas at Austin
- Worked as a cartoonist for *The Daily Texan*, the school newspaper
- Won the National Third Coast Film and Video Festival for his film *Austin Stories*, which earned him entry into the film department at the University of Texas
- His first 16-mm film, *Bedhead*, won several first places among fourteen film festivals
- Financed his first feature-length movie by participating in drug research studies
- 1991, made *El Mariachi* in Mexico with Carlos Gallardo for $7,000
- 1992, signed a movie deal with Columbia Pictures and sold rights to *El Mariachi*
- 1995, Columbia Pictures released *Desperado,* the second of Robert's mariachi trilogies
- Published a book, *Rebel Without a Crew*, in fall of 1995
- 1996, directed *From Dusk Till Dawn*, backed by Miramax Films
- Currently: married to Elizabeth Avellan; they have one son, Rocket Valentino; they live in Austin, Texas, and Los Angeles, California

Robert says that those early days constantly remind him that if you bleed for your money, you will be very careful how you spend it.

ROBERT RODRIGUEZ

In 1989, Robert Rodriguez called the Pharmaco Research Hospital Hotline to inquire about upcoming drug studies. The company hired people to participate in their experimental medical research. Robert heard about several different studies that lasted from a few days to several weeks. They paid varying amounts of money. The hotline mentioned a study coming up that paid $2,000 for a seven-day stay at the facility. This was great, thought Robert. He was sure he had struck gold. Where else could he earn so much money in such a short amount of time?

While Robert was in college, many of his classmates participated in these drug studies to make some extra money. At first, Robert thought this was terrible. Who knew if some of the drugs would fry his brain? But eventually the temptation to earn quick money overtook his reason, and he found himself volunteering to participate in these studies as well. As he likes to say, "I sold my body to science and became a human lab rat for some quick cash."

The first study was not quite what Robert had envisioned. When he checked into the hospital, he found out that the drug they would be testing on him was a speed healing drug. The medicine was supposed to quicken the natural healing process. But, in order to test the new drug, they had to have a wound to heal. So they wounded Robert in two places to see if the new drug would work. They punched out a hole in the back of each of his arms. On one arm, they applied the speed healing drug; on the other, they applied a placebo (a drug that was not expected to speed healing) to see which wound would heal more quickly. Then he was free to wander around the hospital for seven days. At the end of the study, Robert was paid $2,000, and he still has the scars on the backs of his arms to remind him how he used to finance his films.

With his money, Robert paid some tuition bills, bought some books for school, and made a film called *Bedhead*. He says that those early days constantly remind him that if you bleed for your money, you will be very careful how you spend it. His experience taught him how to make movies on a very small budget.

Robert Rodriguez was born on June 20, 1968, in San Antonio, Texas. He was the third child of Rebecca (Villegas) and Cecilio Rodriguez, who eventually had ten children. Cecilio Rodriguez makes his living selling cookware, fine china, and crystal. He has amply provided for his entire family, though money was always tight in such a large family. Robert's grandparents came to the United States from Mexico.

Rebecca and Cecilio Rodriguez have ten children.

ROBERT RODRIGUEZ

Some of
Robert's
earliest
memories
are of the
neighbor-
hood movie
theater.

Robert is the third generation of his family to live in the United States.

Robert's parents were married in 1963, and their first child, Angela, was born the following year. Between 1964 and 1982, they had nine additional children: Cecil, Robert, Patricia, John, Marcel, Elizabeth, David, Rebecca, and Christina. Having a large family had its challenges. There were never enough bedrooms for everyone to have his or her own room. So the younger children slept together in one room, but the teenagers each had separate rooms. As one child moved away to go to college, another child inherited his bedroom. "There was always someone to do stuff with," remembers Robert, "and if I ever got mad at one brother or we had an argument, there was always another brother to go do things with." Regardless of what else his parents were able to give to their children, they felt it was most important to give them a good education. Robert and each of his brothers and sisters attended private Catholic schools.

Some of Robert's earliest memories are of the neighborhood movie theater. Every week, his mother would take all the children to The Olmos Theater to see double and triple features of classic films. Rebecca Rodriguez was suspicious of all the new movies out at that time, and she wanted her children to see only the same movies she had seen when she was growing up. So Robert saw mostly musicals, the Marx Brothers comedies, and an occasional Hitchcock mystery. "We'd sit with food hidden in bags of diapers," recalls Robert, "and watch the movies two or three times."

Robert never paid attention when he was in school. "I wasn't very good in math, science, history . . . in anything really," he says. Since he felt he couldn't do well in school, he often didn't bother trying. While the teacher would drone on about one subject after another, Robert would draw little cartoon characters. "In fifth grade I remember sitting in the back of the class with a paperback dictionary in my hands and using the side margins, where there is no writing, to draw in little stick figures on each page, creating my own little flip cartoon movies," says Robert. "I had the entire day to draw my movies. The elaborate cartoons featured invincible characters bouncing around and off the pages, battling evil, and blowing up everything in sight."

Robert always felt bad that he couldn't do better in school. But he enjoyed the approval he got from the other kids, who would laugh at his paper movies. This made him feel good about himself, so he drew all the time.

When he was in eighth grade, Robert and a few of his friends went to see *Escape from New York*. After the film, they decided they wanted to make their own real movies. The only problem was they had no equipment. "I'd read books about Ray Harryhausen," Robert remembers, "and they said you needed at least a 16-millimeter camera with stop-motion capabilities to do

Robert at about seven years old

Clay animation is the best kind of movie to make when you're younger because you can shoot for hours and your clay actors never complain, they don't ask for food, and they don't need stunt doubles.

ROBERT RODRIGUEZ

animated movies or clay animation. Clay animation is the best kind of movie to make when you're younger because you can shoot for hours and hours and your clay actors never complain, they don't ask for food, and they don't need stunt doubles. My father did have an old super-8 film camera, but it couldn't do stop-motion. So I improvised. I'd tap the shutter and move my clay guy around, but the camera produced an annoying flashing effect. I needed the proper equipment."

Technology finally caught up to Robert's dreams when video cassette recorders and video cameras became available for the consumer. In 1979, Robert's father bought a JVC video cassette recorder that he thought he could make sales presentations with. It was very expensive at the time, so the store that sold him the machine threw in a free video camera to go along with it. The camera was a Quasar that connected to the VCR with a twelve-foot cord. It had no viewfinder and it was completely manual, but Robert was in heaven. He was sure he could make a movie with his dad's new camera.

His father gave him the instructions to figure out how to use the camera, and pretty soon Robert was making clay animation movies and comedies starring his brothers and sisters. Even though he had to look at the TV set to see where he was pointing the camera, and he couldn't move more than twelve feet away from the VCR, Robert had an endless supply of cast and crew among his nine brothers and sisters. Someone was always around, ready to help or act in his movies. His live-action movies looked great. He shot absolutely everything with his father's new camera: his newborn baby sister, family gatherings, a science-fiction comedy kung fu action film—anything he could think of. The new toy occupied his time for an entire year. Making movies with a video camera was very affordable, too. Making movies on an 8-millimeter camera cost about twelve dollars for two and a half minutes of finished film; the video film cost a little less for two

Robert's birthday. There were always lots of kids around to celebrate—and to make movies with.

hours' worth of erasable color picture and sound.

The next year, his father decided to buy another VCR, since Robert had taken control of the first one. "To his surprise (or maybe not), I took that one over as well," recalls Robert. "I had realized that with two VCRs hooked together I could edit by playing my movie on one VCR and recording on the other VCR, using the pause button on the recorder to edit out unwanted material. My editing system was born." From the time Robert was thirteen years old, he would shoot his movies with the video camera, edit them be-

"My short movies were getting so famous that my teachers would let me turn in term movies instead of term papers."

tween two VCRs, and then lay down the sound effects and music over them. For the next ten years, Robert practiced making movies in this manner.

Robert attended a junior seminary called St. Anthony's during his high-school years. The school was right across the street from his house. It was also a boarding school. A lot of children from Mexico attended this school to learn English. The priests at St. Anthony's had a better understanding of Robert than his previous teachers had, and he was allowed to express his creativity instead of following a structured curriculum. He found he did much better in his courses and got better grades.

Robert practiced making movies all through school; the more he practiced, the better his movies got. All of his after-school hours and weekends were spent making movies and cartoons. Everyone at school knew about Robert's movies. "My short movies were getting so famous," says Robert, "that my teachers would let me turn in term movies instead of term papers. No one complained because they knew I was pouring more work, time, dedication, and hours into my movies than if I were writing a hundred term papers. Besides, they were entertaining, they starred my schoolmates, and we'd screen them in class." As a result, Robert never did learn to write very well, but he did learn to visualize, a creative talent he would put to good use later on.

ROBERT RODRIGUEZ

Robert's first job in high school was at a photo lab. He showed his boss some of his cartoons and photographs. His boss thought Robert had creative talent. He told him that he needed to learn the technical aspects of photography. "There are a lot of creative people," he said, "that never get anywhere because they have no technical skills." So Robert decided to learn the technical aspects of photography and film-making that he would need.

In high school, Robert met another young filmmaker, Carlos Gallardo, who would eventually star in several of his short movies. Carlos was a boarding student from Mexico, and since Robert lived across the street from the school, Carlos would visit with the Rodriguez family during the school year. Carlos and Robert would make short action comedies in his backyard on weekends.

During his summer vacations, Robert often visited Carlos in Ciudad Acuña, Mexico, the border town where Carlos lived. They would make movies there as well. The town was a beautiful natural location, and the townspeople soon became used to seeing Carlos and Robert running around with their video camera. "We'd get away with staging elaborate stunts in the middle of a busy street," says Robert.

"Believe it or not," he says, "I actually graduated from high school and miraculously got a scholarship to the University of Texas at Austin. My grades were never very good in school, but

▼▼▼▼▼
Carlos and Robert would make short action comedies in his backyard on weekends.
▲▲▲▲▲▲

Robert
found out
that he
couldn't
apply to
the film
department
until he had
completed
two years of
all math,
science,
history, and
English
classes.
These were
his worst
subjects.

ROBERT RODRIGUEZ

I found myself making the honor roll and getting straight As by my junior year in high school." Robert feels that he received so much validation from friends and family who appreciated his hobby that he became more positive about himself. Because he finally became comfortable with himself through his movies and cartoons, his grades improved.

Rebecca and Cecilio Rodriguez expected all of their children to go to college and get a degree. Robert figured the only thing he could ever get a degree in was film, so, because he got a scholarship and there was a film program there, Robert enrolled at the University of Texas.

He was in for a shock, however. Robert found out that he couldn't apply to the film department until he had completed two years of all math, science, history, and English classes. These were his worst subjects. His grade point average (GPA) at the university started out bad and got worse. By the time he had finished his two years, his GPA was so low that he couldn't get into the film department. "The film classes are so small (fewer than thirty seats), and so many people are trying to get into them (more than 200), that the school chooses their film students by their grade point average," recalls Robert. "There were a lot of academic types who got into film classes but made horrible movies. I was one of the many creative types with low GPAs stuck on the outside looking in."

This small setback didn't deter Robert, however. While he tried to get his grades back up, he applied for a job as a cartoonist at *The Daily Texan*, the school newspaper. He got the job and started *Los Hooligans*, a comic strip based on his youngest sister, Christina, that became very popular. He named the character in his comic strip Mari-Carmen. "I would show Christina my comic strips," says Robert, "and tell her that they were about her. She was just a youngster at the time and she was never very impressed." But others were. His comic strips led to other job opportunities. Robert continued to make short movies on his own and entered them in a few video festivals.

In 1988, while he was in school, Robert met Elizabeth Avellan. Born in Caracas, Venezuela, she had moved with her family to Houston in 1974 when her father decided to go back to school in the United States. She also came from a large family: she was the second child and had six brothers and sisters. She had been a full-time student in film production, art, and architecture at Rice University for several years, but her father agreed to pay her college tuition only if she majored in architecture. She did that for three years, but that was not what Elizabeth wanted to do. "Eventually I couldn't fool my father anymore," says Elizabeth. "I didn't want to continue in architecture and he wouldn't pay my tuition. So I dropped out of school, moved to Austin in 1986, and found a full-time job work-

▼▼▼▼▼
In 1988, while he was in school, Robert met Elizabeth Avellan.
▲▲▲▲▲▲

"In school
they don't
teach you
how to
make a
movie when
you have no
money and
no crew."

ing in the vice president's office at the University of Texas. I was able to take a few courses each semester to continue toward my degree. I met Robert when he became a student worker in the same office. He was working three jobs at the time: he had his job on the school newspaper, he was freelancing for a T-shirt company doing drawings, and then he got a job in the office. Robert showed me one of the films he had made of his brothers and sisters. I knew right away that he was incredibly talented. I couldn't believe what he had been able to accomplish."

Most of their dates consisted of watching the movies Robert had directed. Elizabeth loved Robert's films and encouraged him to keep making them and entering them in contests. She was very impressed by his extraordinary storytelling abilities and his talent as a filmmaker. On January 9, 1990, Elizabeth and Robert were married.

Robert was always so busy writing, making, and editing his movies, plus working and going to school, that he never thought about too much else. It was Elizabeth who would watch the newspapers for word about film festivals and video contests. She was constantly reminding him to enter each one. One day, Robert entered his film, *Austin Stories*, in the National Third Coast Film and Video Festival based in Austin. Many students from the University of Texas film department entered also. But Robert was the one who took first place. After he won his award, he took his film to Steve Mims, the film professor who taught Production I, and asked if he would let him take his class in spite of his grades. "He saw my movie and let me in the class," remembers Robert.

Before school began that year, Robert felt he had a big chance to make an award-winning film on 16 millimeter and get himself some recognition. "I shot my movie, pouring every idea and camera trick I could think of into it, and my eight-minute film, *Bedhead*, was born. It won several first places among the fourteen film festivals I sent it to," he says. The film cost $800 to make—money Robert had earned from his participation in the drug study at Pharmaco. The film featured his siblings, his parents' house, his sister's bike, and his brother's skateboard.

Robert's experience with the college film department was somewhat disheartening. "In school they don't teach you how to make a movie when you have no money and no crew. They teach you how to make a movie with a big crew so that when you graduate you can go to Hollywood and get a job pulling cables on someone else's movie," he says. "Or they

Robert and Elizabeth have made an ideal partnership from the beginning.

▼▼▼▼▼
He invented
his own film
school
where he
was the
only student
and where
experiences,
mistakes,
problems,
and
solutions
would be
his teachers.
▲▲▲▲▲▲

teach you how to make contacts. They say that the only way into the business is by knowing people. It's not what you can do, it's who you know. That might get you through the door, but it won't keep you there.

"I was never big on writing scripts," he continues. "I have read many times that the best way to learn is to sit down and write two full scripts, and after you are done, you should throw them away. Then you should start to write your real script. Whoever thought of that game is whacked. It might make sense to get your bad movies out of the way as soon as possible, but I could never bring myself to do all that work just to throw it away. So, instead of writing two scripts and throwing them away, I decided to make them for really low budgets and sell them into the Spanish home-video market where no one in the movie business would see them if they were no good. It was almost like throwing them away, only I would get paid for them. Then after I had done a couple of these low-budget films, I'd have so much experience and confidence, I could explode onto the American independent scene and pretend like I had never made anything before in my life."

This was Robert's motivation to film a Mariachi trilogy with no crew whatsoever. He invented his own film school where he was the only student and where experiences, mistakes, problems, and solutions would be his teachers. In March 1991, Robert got the idea to sell his movie to the Spanish home-video market after he got a call from his friend Carlos Gallardo. Carlos wanted him to come to Mexico to see a film being made in his hometown. It was the biggest-budget movie ever to be made in Mexico. It was the film version of the best-selling Mexican novel *Like Water for Chocolate,* and it was being shot in Ciudad Acuña by Alfonso Arau. Arau asked Carlos to help with production since he was familiar with the town. So over spring break, Robert went to visit Carlos and shot some behind-the-scenes footage of what later went on to become one of the most popular Mexican movies in recent years.

Robert went back to school with renewed enthusiasm. He made his first 16-mm color short film at school and made plans for filming *El Mariachi* in the summer. Then, one day, one of his film-school teachers asked what he would be doing that summer. Robert told him about his idea for

Robert on his wedding day in January 1990

ROBERT RODRIGUEZ

El Mariachi. "Who's your director of photography?" his teacher asked.

Robert stopped. He was afraid to tell him he was planning to do the whole thing by himself, without a crew, so he said, "Well, I'll be the director of photography, but I'll probably have a small crew around to help out."

"No, no, no," his teacher said, "you're going to fail! Your actors are going to hate you! They're going to be sitting there waiting for you while you light the set. Don't be an idiot! Get a director of photography. You have to learn how to delegate."

Robert was determined to do everything on the movie by himself. He could not afford to hire a crew. Even if they worked for free, he would have to feed them, and that would cost more money than he had. Robert was determined that he and Carlos could find the actors and shoot the entire movie themselves, with no other help. Carlos made plans to look for a camera they could borrow, and Robert began to think of ways he could raise money for the film and write the script.

Robert immediately thought of Pharmaco. They had a drug study coming up that paid $3,000, but it would require that he stay at the facility for one whole month. Robert thought this would be perfect. He'd have nothing better to do while he was locked away than to write a feature-length script for his first Mariachi film. In his mind, Robert imagined he was getting paid

Robert was determined that he and Carlos could find the actors and shoot the entire movie themselves, with no other help.

to write his script, which made the whole thing easier for him to accept. The only problem was that the competition for this study was pretty stiff. There were forty other guys competing for the study, and only twenty people would be accepted. In order to be accepted, Robert had to pass a physical, and the company had to be convinced that he was in top physical condition.

On May 31, 1991, Robert checked into the research hospital prepared to spend one month alone, writing his script. At the facility, he met Peter Marquardt, and the two became friends. Robert told Peter about his Mariachi film. Peter told Robert he had always wanted to be in a movie. "I told him he could play the bad guy if he wanted to," says Robert. Peter wanted to.

Through all of June, Robert sketched out his script on index cards. His idea was to have a good guy, the mariachi, and a bad guy, named Azul, who sort of resemble each other. The mariachi arrives at a bar in Mexico looking for work. He is dressed in black and carries a guitar case. When he finds no job at the bar, he leaves. Then Azul follows, also carrying a guitar case. Only his guitar case is filled with guns. Azul orders a beer, walks up to a table with some other bad guys, shoots them all dead, and leaves. The bartender tries to call the cops, but then Azul comes back. The bartender is sure Azul will kill him next. But Azul pays for his beer and leaves. As the mariachi proceeds to the next bar looking for work, someone mistakes him for Azul. Carlos

▼▼▼▼▼
Through all of June, Robert sketched out his script on index cards.
▲▲▲▲▲▲

was going to play the mariachi, and his friend Reinol Martinez would be Azul. By July 3, Robert had finished his script, and his stay at the research hospital was over. He had a lot to do in what remained of the summer.

Carlos and Robert had to find a camera they could afford, or borrow one. The good ones they wanted were too expensive to buy or rent, so Robert asked his good friend Keith if they could borrow his 16-mm camera for a while. Keith said yes. Robert and Carlos then went down to Mexico to scout out locations to shoot the film. Robert decided that shooting in Mexico was much more reasonable than shooting in the United States. They were much more likely to tolerate people running around in the streets with cameras than there in Texas.

Carlos found a great jail they could use, and the two went to look it over and plan their shots. Carlos asked the chief at the jail if they had any machine guns. The chief had a Mac-10, which he let Carlos practice shooting outside. Carlos said they could get permission from the mayor to borrow some guns, as long as the cops were around when they fired them. That's probably something they couldn't do in Texas.

It turned out that Robert was able to borrow the camera for only three weeks, and he had only $7,000 spend. This would buy nothing more than film and developing.

It was so hot on July 31, 1991, when they began shooting the movie that Robert had sweat

Robert and Carlos then went down to Mexico to scout out locations to shoot the film.

dripping on the film as he loaded it into the camera. They cast many townspeople in the film so that the people would be more tolerant of their taking over the town for a couple of weeks. Robert could not afford money for costumes, so he had to pick clothes from his actors' wardrobes to use. Each day, he would shoot as many scenes as possible, then spend the rest of the day planning for the next day's shoot. He stayed with Carlos's family while he was in Mexico.

Robert had so much fun filming his movie that time passed very quickly. In early August, Carlos got the local cops to help with their gun scene. The cops stopped traffic for them and helped them fire the guns. They could not afford prop guns and were using real guns with blanks as bullets. But the blanks didn't have as much force as real bullets, and they would jam the guns when they were fired. Robert had to do an amazing editing job later to make it look like the bad guys had semiautomatic weapons when all they could fire was one shot at a time.

One day, the authorities let them borrow the jail. While they were filming, one of the real prisoners was being so loud that the guard took him outside so that he wouldn't disturb production. The prisoner escaped! They caught him an hour or so later not far from town.

On August 7, Robert's friend Peter from the research hospital came down to Mexico to shoot his scenes. He was so happy to be in a real movie. But when Robert handed him his lines

▼▼▼▼▼▼
One day, the authorities let them borrow the jail. While they were filming, one of the real prisoners was being so loud that the guard took him outside. The prisoner escaped!
▲▲▲▲▲▲

49

One very difficult task Robert faced in putting his movie together was getting his sound to sync.

for the next day's shoot, Peter turned pale. All his lines were in Spanish, and Peter couldn't speak a word of Spanish! Robert had to teach Peter each line phonetically, and Peter had no idea what he was saying. So Robert put sunglasses on him and gave him cheat notes to read from. Peter is staring down at his notes behind his sunglasses in all his scenes.

By August 20, the camera had to be returned. Robert had finished shooting as much as he could. By then he had shot 25 rolls of film. Then the real work began. Robert had to edit all the scenes together into a movie. To save money, he had shot only one take of each scene. If that take didn't turn out, there was nothing he could do about it. He returned to Austin to borrow some editing equipment.

One very difficult task Robert faced in putting his movie together was getting his sound to sync. If he had been able to obtain more modern camera equipment, he would have shot the movie with sound. But his camera did not have sound. So when he edited the film to video, he had to record the sound on a tape recorder and match it up with the actors' mouths moving onscreen. This was very difficult and time consuming. Often an entire scene would not sync, so Robert had to cut away from the actor so the audience would just hear the dialog but not see the actor's mouth moving. He ended up with two thousand cuts in his film. By Thanksgiving, Robert had finished *El Mariachi.*

Elizabeth wanted to see the movie. In all this time, she had been finishing her college degree and had never seen any of it. Finally he showed it to her. "What do you think?" Robert cautiously asked her.

"Well, I give it three and a half stars for the movie itself. But then, knowing all the insane work you put into it, and considering you did it with no crew and old equipment and very little money, I give it five stars," answered Elizabeth. Robert was happy with her answer but afraid she might be biased. After all, she was his wife!

Robert wanted to sell his film so that he could earn a profit and make a sequel. On December 1,

Robert shooting *El Mariachi*. He is giving instructions to Carlos Gallardo.

Carlos and Robert headed for Los Angeles to look for a distributor. They also decided to look for an agent at International Creative Management (ICM) while they were in California. They hoped to have the film sold and be back home by Christmas. They drove all the way from Texas to Los Angeles. It took them nearly 24 hours to complete their trip. They stayed with a friend who had an apartment and let them sleep on the floor. Robert and Carlos had no money for hotels.

ROBERT RODRIGUEZ

Though many of the company executives seemed interested, no one made an offer for the film.

Robert had made a list of companies he wanted to try to sell his film to. Carlos and Robert rented Spanish home videos and copied the company information from each one. Each day they called on a different company and tried to get to see someone with authority to purchase their film. They went to Film-Mex, Mex-American, Million Dollar Video, Tel-Star, and Cine-Mex. Though many of the company executives seemed interested, no one made an offer for the film. Then, finally, Mex-American offered them $25,000 for the movie! Robert was thrilled, but he wanted to see if he could get a better offer. He was hoping to get $35,000 or $40,000 at least. He went on to visit MexCinema, where they offered him $10,000 and a share of the profits. Robert then decided that the Mex-American offer might be the best he'd get, so he accepted it. He called them and told them to get the check ready.

Robert also looked into some other business while he was in Los Angeles. A friend had told him to stop by ICM and talk to Robert Newman, a talent agent. He called Mr. Newman's office and spoke to his assistant, Warren. Robert wanted to show Newman his demo tape. He dropped off his tape and was told that Mr. Newman would be in touch with him after he viewed the film. Two days later, Robert Newman's office called. Mr. Newman had tried to watch the tape, but his VCR ate it! Robert had to make another one and bring it back. When he went to deliver it, he was surprised that Mr. Newman would meet with him. Robert told him how he made his film and what his plans for the future were. The following week, Mr. Newman called Robert to tell him he wanted to work with him. Robert Newman would represent Robert Rodriguez. As his agent, Mr. Newman would look out for Robert's interests.

As it turned out, the Mex-American contract for Robert's movie was not really what it seemed to be. When Robert went to pick up the contract, there was a check for $10,000, not $25,000, as they had offered. They told Robert that the $10,000 was for U.S. rights only. They had a sister company in Mexico that was putting up the other $15,000 for Mexican rights. Robert would have to wait for the other check from Mexico. Robert didn't want to sell just U.S. rights without Mexican rights. He wouldn't sell his movie until he received all his money. Robert and Carlos had to return home without having sold their film. It was nearly Christmas, and they couldn't be away any longer. They packed up and returned home empty-handed.

They really didn't go home empty-handed. Robert Newman, Robert's new agent, began getting him a lot of publicity. ICM showed his movie around. His life moved into fast-forward after this. Pretty soon, many companies were interested in him, including Disney, Columbia, Tri-Star, and Miramax Films. They all wanted him to come work for them. Each one talked to him

▼▼▼▼▼
Pretty soon, many companies were interested in Robert, including Disney, Columbia, Tri-Star, and Miramax Films. They all wanted him to come work for them.
▲▲▲▲▲▲

In the end, Columbia Pictures offered Robert a two-year movie deal with the chance to make additional films.

about what he'd like to do next. They paid for his airfare to and from Los Angeles now. He didn't have to drive anymore. When he was there, they put him up in nice hotels and took him out for expensive meals. Some companies suggested remaking *El Mariachi* to release in the theaters. Some suggested making a sequel. Some wanted to change his film from a mainly Latino cast to one that included more Anglos. In the end, Columbia Pictures offered Robert a two-year movie deal with the chance to make additional films, plus they wanted to buy the rights to his $7,000 movie and screen it for possible release to theaters nationwide. Robert had his foot in Hollywood.

"*El Mariachi* opened with a bang and fell off quietly. It did much better than I had imagined, fueled mainly by the wonderful ad campaign that Columbia put out with the film," Robert tells us. "Later in the year, it was released on videotape, where it lives on today. It was strange finally holding my own video box cover in my hand. I never would have entertained the idea that *El Mariachi* was going to be my breakthrough film. I thought it was just a practice film so one day I could make great movies."

Because of all the publicity surrounding *El Mariachi*, Robert did not get behind a camera again until January 1994. But then he didn't stop. He wrote, directed, and edited three movies in 1994, then directed and edited another one in the summer of 1995. The first movie he made in 1994 was called *Roadracers*, and he made this movie for cable TV's Showtime. Later that year, he returned to Mexico to make the next Mariachi adventure, which he called *Pistolero*. The studio renamed it *Desperado* and gave him a $7-million budget. This time, Robert could have actors and actresses that everyone would recognize. Antonio Banderas, Mexican superstar Salma Hayek, and Academy Award-winning screenwriter Quentin Tarantino were featured in the film. The movie was released in August 1995.

Robert wrote, directed, produced, and often donned the Steadicam on the set of his movie *Desperado*.

To Robert, it was the realization of a childhood dream: an action film starring Hispanic actors. He also had a predominantly Hispanic crew. More than 80 percent of the crew was Mexican, which, according to Columbia, is the highest percentage of Mexican technical talent ever used on a film for an American company.

In *Desperado*, Banderas tracks down a Mexican drug lord. "I wanted to take my seven-million-dollar budget," Robert says, "and make it look like the film cost thirty million. I wanted to take a modest budget by Hollywood standards and show them what

▼▼▼▼▼▼

More than
80 percent
of the crew
was
Mexican,
which,
according to
Columbia, is
the highest
percentage
of Mexican
technical
talent ever
used on a
film for an
American
company.
▲▲▲▲▲▲

ROBERT RODRIGUEZ

they could do with their money. I was used to tight budgets."

To save time and money, Robert filled his home with rented sound and editing equipment. Three sound editors, two assistant editors, and an apprentice worked all hours in his house. Robert said it felt like old times. Both Elizabeth and he were used to having people all over the house.

A week after wrapping up *Desperado*, Robert ran off to write, direct, and edit a segment of the movie *Four Rooms* with codirectors Quentin Tarantino and Alex Rockwell. The comedy has four plots. Each director wrote a 30-minute block of the movie, each one about characters staying in different rooms of the same hotel. A bellhop weaves the action together. The movie features Madonna, Tim Roth, and Marisa Tomei. Robert cast Antonio Banderas and Tamlyn Tomita in his portion of the film, which he calls "the Mexican room."

Next, Robert directed *From Dusk Till Dawn*, which was backed by Miramax Films and starred George Clooney, Quentin Tarantino, and Cheech Marin. In this movie, the notorious Gecko Brothers, two of America's most dangerous criminals, are on the run from the Texas police and the FBI after a crime spree through the Southwest. Their chances of survival don't look too bright on the home front. But across the border in Mexico, the mysterious Carlos offers them sanctuary in return for some of their ill-gotten goods.

ROBERT RODRIGUEZ

In the fall of 1995, Dutton published Robert's book, *Rebel Without a Crew*, which documents his making of the first mariachi adventure. Just prior to the release of *From Dusk Till Dawn*, Robert closed a deal with Sony/Epic to create his own label, Los Hooligans Records. Beginning with the music from *From Dusk Till Dawn*, he will release his own movie sound tracks in addition to signing bands. Robert has a contract to do two more movies with Miramax films that he will control. He is also writing a feature film for Fox called *Predators*.

Robert on location for his movie *From Dusk Till Dawn*

With all his amazing accomplishments, Robert has not yet had a chance to finish his college degree. His fame came just two credits shy of graduation. (The University of Texas has invited Robert to teach a college course in exchange for the two credits he needs for his degree.) But Elizabeth did finally earn her degree from Rice University about the time that Robert signed his first contract with Columbia Pictures. On September 14, 1995, Robert and Elizabeth had a baby boy, Rocket Valentino Avellan Rodriguez. Amid the hustle and bustle of Robert's stardom, he still maintains a very down-to-earth attitude. "*El Mariachi* actually turned out to be more mythical than I ever imagined," he says. "And that little taste of glory after years of hard work was a lot closer than I was ever led to believe. Success in this business is not an impossible dream."

Robert and Elizabeth rented a big house in Los Angeles so that they would have a place to stay when Robert is making films there. He has rooms full of editing equipment so that he can edit all night long when he wants to. Back in Austin, they bought 60 acres of land on which to build a new home; it will also house Robert's office. Robert and Elizabeth plan to have a big family like the ones they each came from. They don't believe that a home is a building. "A home is where the love is," they say. And Robert takes his family with him wherever he goes. Elizabeth and Rocket travel nearly everywhere that Robert's business

Robert and Elizabeth with baby Rocket

takes him. Elizabeth coproduces many of Robert's films.

Elizabeth provides some insight into her husband's success. "Robert has always marched to his own drummer," she says. "In addition to the fact that he is incredibly talented, he never succumbed to peer pressure. Robert doesn't live for the publicity. He's very quiet; he's always listening, always thinking. He knows exactly what he wants to do and he isn't impressed by all the dazzle of Hollywood. He doesn't drink, he doesn't smoke, and he never has. He has always wanted to do something with his life, and while most of his other friends were out partying, he was working at making films. It never bothered him that he was different; he always knew what he wanted to do when his friends were just out wasting time."

Robert says that he has always enjoyed creating things. He loved to do drawings when he was younger so that he could show them to his friends and siblings. That's also what he enjoys so much about making movies. He can provide enjoyment and entertainment for others. "Actually, making movies for the big production companies is not much different from making the movies I made for myself," says Robert. "I had fun directing my friends and family who starred in my movies several years ago. Now the movie stars have become my friends, and I have fun with them, too. Of course, there is more responsibility involved in making multimillion-dollar

Elizabeth and Rocket travel nearly everywhere that Robert's business takes him. Elizabeth coproduces many of Robert's films.

ROBERT RODRIGUEZ

The Rodriguez family from left to right: (back row) Jon, Robert, Marcel, father Cecilio, Cecil, David, (front row) mother Rebecca, Patricia, Rebecca, Elizabeth, Angela, and Christina

pictures, but I still enjoy it just the same. I think if you enjoy what you do, it'll really come through in your work. I didn't do this to become famous or rich. In fact, I really thought I'd just be a bum, because I had never really found something I could make a career out of. My parents were very supportive of whatever I wanted to do, from giving me music lessons to art lessons. But I never seemed to have any talent in much of anything. Making films became my passion, and it's funny how things turned out. My passion has become my career."

ROBERT RODRIGUEZ

From the time Robert was small, he has always kept a journal. Each night he writes down everything he accomplishes during the day. Years ago, his father told him that he should be aware of what he does with his time. If he didn't accomplish something important every day, he would be throwing his life away. When Robert keeps his diary, he can see exactly what he did with his time. But his journal has provided a learning experience for him as well. On some days, Robert was disappointed with the turn of events. Weeks later, he was able to look back at everything that had happened and see that many times, things turn out for the best. Writing a diary allows Robert to know where he's been and to plan where he's going.

Robert does not operate like most other Hollywood film directors. He still likes to do most everything himself. Though writing is his least favorite aspect of making movies, Elizabeth says that he writes movies so that he can have something cool to shoot. "He runs the main camera himself so he can have something cool to edit. He loves editing the best, but he doesn't want to just edit what someone else has shot.

"Robert is so levelheaded," says Elizabeth. "He dedicates his life to accomplishing things. He's very focused; he's very disciplined; yet, when he was in school, many teachers thought he would just be a loser. You can't always tell by school grades how well someone will do in life."

▼▼▼▼▼
Robert does not operate like most other Hollywood film directors. He still likes to do most everything himself.
▲▲▲▲▲▲

JOSEFINA LÓPEZ

Playwright, Film and TV Writer, Producer, Actress
1969-

"Any feeling you feel is perfectly good. There is no such thing as a wrong or bad feeling. Anger is good. Don't let anyone tell you you have no right to be angry. Anger is what we sometimes call passion. Anger is what allows us to challenge injustice. If you don't like something, you have all the power within you to change it. If you focus and channel all your anger into something positive, you can do amazing things; you may even be able to change the world.**"**

Josefina López, as told to Barbara Marvis, March 1996

BIO HIGHLIGHTS

- Born March 19, 1969, in Cerritos, San Luis Potosí, Mexico; mother: Catalina Perales López; father: Rosendo Z. López
- Grew up in Boyle Heights in East Los Angeles, California
- Wrote first hit one-act play, *Simply Maria, or The American Dream*, at 17 while in high school
- 1987, graduated from the Los Angeles County High School for the Arts in Monterey Park, California
- At 19, wrote first full-length play, *Real Women Have Curves*, 1988
- PBS production of *Simply Maria* won Emmy for Outstanding Achievement Entertainment Program, September 1989
- At 23, wrote *Unconquered Spirits*, a historical dramatic play
- February 1993, won *USA Today* award for creativity outside the classroom
- Received scholarship from Columbia College in Chicago and graduated with honors and a B.A. in Film and Screenwriting in May of 1993
- At 25, wrote *Confessions of Women from East L.A.*
- Became a U.S. citizen on November 9, 1995
- Currently: single; resides in West Hollywood, California

Not having
the papers
that
declared she
could
legally
reside in
the United
States,
Josefina
grew up in
fear . . .

JOSEFINA LÓPEZ

When Josefina López was a small girl in East Los Angeles, she was in an uncomfortable, frightening position. She, along with some of her eight brothers and sisters, was an undocumented immigrant. Her father and mother were legal residents and had permission to live in the United States. But several of their children did not. The family spoke only Spanish at home and they did not understand all the documentation requirements. Not having the papers that declared she could legally reside in the United States, Josefina grew up in fear, worried that someday someone would notice she was undocumented and would send her back to Mexico.

But today things are much better for Josefina. She is currently the most produced Latina playwright in the country and one of the most successful. As well as penning plays, she writes screenplays for television and movies, acts in some of her plays, and writes for magazines. And, at the age of 26, in November 1995, she became a U.S. citizen, a moment of which she is very proud.

Josefina was born on March 19, 1969, in Cerritos, San Luis Potosí, Mexico. She came to the U.S. with her parents and her younger sister when she was five years old. Since her father, Rosendo Z. López, couldn't find a job in Mexico, he was participating in the *bracero* program, which was a worker-exchange program for U.S. agricultural businesses needing laborers. After several years, he had earned enough money to bring the rest of the family to the United States, and he and his wife became legal residents. Josefina's mother, Catalina Perales López, earned money as a seamstress.

In Mexico during the 1950s, says Josefina, "My parents didn't have the opportunity to have a career. My father would herd sheep, tend cornfields, and do other things on his parents' farm." Rosendo and Catalina were introduced to each other one day at a friend's house. They fell in love at first sight and began a long courtship, during which they wrote letters to one another. Through these letters, Rosendo and Catalina decided to elope.

The young couple's family grew quickly, and they had six of their eight children in Mexico: Juan in 1959, Rosaura in 1961, Esther in 1963, Carmen in 1965, Rosendo, Jr., in 1967, and Josefina in 1969. Trying to support the family was difficult; good jobs were scarce in San Luis Potosí. Rosendo had heard about opportunities for campesinos, or farmworkers, far to the north. The López family emigrated to the United States and settled in Los Angeles. The youngest children: Angelica, born in 1972, and Fernando,

Josefina is just three months old, shown here in her mother's arms. From left to right (back): father Rosendo; Rosendo, Jr. (front) Juan, Rosaura, Carmen, and Esther, taken in 1969.

JOSEFINA LÓPEZ

born in 1979, were both born in California, so they automatically became U.S. citizens.

Although Josefina draws heavily on her childhood and upbringing for material for her plays, she says, "My mother doesn't like me writing about her or my family. Almost all of my writing so far has been autobiographical, and I've written about my mother so many times, she's jokingly threatened to sue me if I write about her again. I can't help writing about my mother because she's such an inspiration to me! She is a bundle of contradictions. She's very funny and she's very wise."

In an essay titled "On Being a Playwright," which Josefina wrote for *Ollantay Theater Magazine* in 1993, she described the influence of her mother on her writing: "My first story was about a little feminist ant who built her own house by herself. My parents would ask me to tell it to our relatives, and after they heard it they would always tell me I was a good storyteller. I learned this from my mother, who was my first teacher of writing. She tells the best stories and the juiciest gossip. Any little *chisme* (gossip) she'll find the gasps, and the exag-

Josefina's parents, Catalina and Rosendo López

gerations, and the gestures, and the eyes, *y todo* (and everything). I remember when some nights my family would sit around the living room listening to my mother tell stories about *La Llorona, duendes,* skeletons, and the devil. I would be so scared, but I have always loved a good story."

An imaginative child, Josefina picked up on the storytelling tradition perpetuated by her mother and would often tell tales and produce plays in the backyard for the amusement of her extended family. "My parents would often call me crazy—*loquita,* or *La Locadia*— which would bother me very much. I was always the wild one. My parents thought I was 'so dramatic.'

Josefina at eleven years old

They were afraid I was going to end up like my father's crazy aunt. . . . They didn't understand that I was actually talented and not just crazy. They never told me not to be a writer or an actress; they stayed out of my way. They were often worried that I was too ambitious."

Josefina was eventually able to understand her parents, and they eventually accepted her. "Today my parents are much more accepting of me and my talent," she continues. "I'm the person I am today as a result of my father's ambi-

JOSEFINA LÓPEZ

Josefina's high-school prom picture

tious spirit and my mother's generosity and understanding of others. My parents didn't give me a lot of material things because they didn't have them, but they gave me their stories. I owe a lot to them for that."

Josefina's education began in 1976 at Breed Street Elementary in Boyle Heights, California, a predominantly Latino district of Los Angeles. She remembers how when she was very young, her parents warned her not to tell anyone she didn't have *papeles* (papers).

One time, she and her best friend were walking to the corner store, being vigilant, as usual. As Josefina remembers it: "On the way to the store, we saw *la migra* (the immigration authorities). I quickly turned to my friend and tried to 'act white.' I spoke in English and talked about Jordache jeans and Barbie dolls, hoping no one would suspect us. When I finally got my legal residence card, I remembered this incident, knowing that I would never have to hide and be afraid again. I also laughed at my naïveté and fear, because what I had thought was *la migra* was only an L.A. meter maid."

Josefina attended Hollenbeck Junior High School in Boyle Heights and enrolled in Roosevelt High School in 1984. There were lots of students whose culture was similar to hers, but she was still undocumented and was therefore unsure if she actually belonged or was considered a foreigner. In addition, she hadn't yet found a place to vent her conflicting emotions.

JOSEFINA LÓPEZ

On the other hand, the Los Angeles County High School for the Arts in Monterey Park, California, would turn out to be the kind of place she could fit in and hone her creative skills. Inspired by the movie *Fame*, Josefina wanted badly to go to an arts high school and become an actress. She applied to and was accepted at the Los Angeles County High School for the Arts, from which she graduated in 1987.

High school is a confusing time for most teenagers, but for Josefina it was doubly so because of the two cultures clashing in her mind. Looking back on that time, she told a reporter for the *Dallas Observer*, "My parents were applying the rules of Mexico to me. Here I was, surrounded by American culture, I could see I could go to college, there were so many things I could do. . . . I was feeling so much anger and confusion, I decided to write about it instead of doing something destructive. It was the only thing I could think to do."

In 1989, while in high school, Josefina met her

Josefina with playwright Luis Valdez, the father of Chicano theater

role model, playwright Luis Valdez, acknowledged as "the Father of Chicano theater" and the founder of *El Teatro Campesino*. Valdez's grassroots theater troupe was originally formed in the 1960s to entertain and educate migrant farmworkers about the value of unionization. Josefina saw Valdez's play *La Carpa* (*La Gran Carpa de la Familia Rascuachi*) in ninth grade and *I Don't Have to Show You No Stinking Badges* when she was a junior. Speaking of *Badges*, Josefina says, "I loved it because it mentioned the word 'López,' and the fact that these characters had last names that were Latino, Mexican, was such a big deal to me because I had never seen anything . . . remotely close to what I had been through."

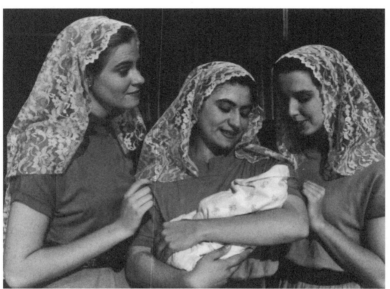

A 1988 production of *Simply Maria*. This scene shows Maria and her three angels.

Valdez's play *Badges* told a story about racism in Hollywood. After watching the play, Josefina concluded that she couldn't get a job as an actress, and that was what planted the seed that she should write Latina female roles herself. Yet, besides being positively influenced to pursue a career as a playwright, she also received the strong message that women—particularly Latinas—weren't adequately represented in theater. She kept looking for significant Latina roles in plays. Finding none, even in the plays of Luis Valdez, Josefina says, "I figured out that even Luis Valdez can't do it all. We can't expect him to write every story, because he can't; we need more writers, and we also need more writers for women, because [real Latinas] are neither virgins, mothers, nor whores. As a Latina, I'm much more complex than that. So I thought, 'Well, I better do something if I can do something,' and so I tried. I started writing."

When she was a junior in high school, she wrote her first play, *Simply Maria, or Something to Cut*, and later retitled *Simply Maria, or The American Dream*. The one-act play and its reception marked the beginning of her professional writing career. Responding to a challenge from her high-school playwriting teacher, she submitted *Simply Maria* to the Young Playwrights Festival of New York. She won a free trip to New York City, where the play had a public reading by professional actors. Then she found out about a workshop for Latino playwrights with Irene Forbes, also in New York, for which she was selected to participate.

Simply Maria took on a life of its own. After Josefina graduated from high school, the play won the California Young Playwrights Project out of 169 entries. It was produced at the Gaslamp Quarter Theater for six performances in 1988. In

▼▼▼▼▼

When she was a junior in high school, she wrote her first play, *Simply Maria*.

▲▲▲▲▲▲

JOSEFINA LÓPEZ

Valdez has called Josefina López "one of the most brilliant young voices writing for the theater in this country today."

1989, the play was produced for PBS as a co-production between the Playwrights Project and KPBS in San Diego. It aired during Hispanic Heritage Month in September 1989. The PBS production won an Emmy for Outstanding Achievement Entertainment Program; a Gold Award from the Corporation of Public Broadcasting, Children's Category; and a Media Award from the Conference of Christians and Jews for "Promoting Cultural Understanding."

Josefina eventually was recognized by her role model. In 1990, Luis Valdez's *El Teatro Campesino* took *Simply Maria* on the road. It toured for four years, playing in 40 cities and 25 states. Valdez has called Josefina López "one of the most brilliant young voices writing for the theater in this country today."

During her senior year in high school, Josefina had a major crisis in her life. She was trying to figure out how she could go to college. Her parents were unable to pay for it, she knew. Even worse, she realized that being undocumented made her ineligible for any scholarships or grants for college. Without financial aid, Josefina could not attend college. Soon after graduation, she applied for amnesty and got a residence card. This made her eligible to apply for college. She was accepted at New York University but had to wait a year to be eligible for financial aid. During that year she worked at McDonald's and at her sister's tiny sewing factory. Her experiences there served as the inspi-

Josefina López

The cast and crew of *Real Women Have Curves* celebrated Josefina's 25th birthday on March 19, 1994, at the San Diego Repertory Theatre.

ration for her next play, *Real Women Have Curves*, written when she was 19.

Real Women is a full-length play about five Mexican-American women who toil in a small sewing factory in East Los Angeles. They are trying to finish a large dress order to save the factory from financial ruin. At the same time, they are in hiding from the Immigration and Naturalization Service. The women are closed up in the sweltering heat of the tiny sewing factory, afraid of losing their jobs if the factory is forced to close. They keep each other's spirits up by dreaming of owning their own dress boutique one day, which won't make dresses for women

▼▼▼▼▼

"I had to drop out of college three times because I ran out of money," says Josefina.

▲▲▲▲▲▲

who wear size three, but for "real women with curves." The camaraderie and sisterhood of the five seamstresses lead to their discovery that in their world, they provide hope for each other. By 1996, *Real Women Have Curves* has had 17 productions with a total of 419 performances and had grossed over $1 million.

Josefina's experiences as an undocumented resident make her very sad about the way undocumented immigrants have been treated in this country. The children of poor people who come to this country for economic opportunity do not choose to be "law-breakers." She says, emphatically, "In the United States, undocumented people are referred to as 'illegal aliens,' which conjures up in our minds the image of extraterrestrial beings who are not human, who do not bleed when they are cut, who do not cry when they feel pain, who do not have fears, dreams, and hopes. Undocumented people have been used as scapegoats for so many of the problems in the U.S.—from drugs to violence to the economy. I hope that someday this country recognizes the very important contributions of undocumented people and remembers that they too came to this country in search of a better life."

Attending New York University's Tisch School of the Arts exposed Josefina to New York City life, especially its art and theater scene. During her freshman year, she lived modestly and worked on a degree in dramatic writing. Then, unable to pay the tuition, she transferred to the

Josefina López

University of California at San Diego for her sophomore year, followed by two semesters at East Los Angeles College. After working to accumulate funds, she enrolled in Columbia College in Chicago, Illinois.

It was very hard for Josefina to finish college because of the financial burden. She says, "I had to drop out of college three times because I ran out of money. I was always so stressed out for money that I couldn't sleep or concentrate on my schoolwork. I gave up once for that very reason, but decided to continue a year later."

There was hope just around the corner. In her senior year at Columbia College, she again dropped out due to lack of money and left Chicago to go to a community college in California. During that fall, she applied for a scholarship sponsored by a national newspaper, *USA Today*. It turned out to be just the break she needed. She was one out of twenty scholarship winners across the nation for "creativity outside the classroom."

Josefina went to Washington, D.C. to receive her All-USA College Academic Team Award from *USA Today* in February 1993.

"The *USA Today* scholarship was tailor-made for me," she explains. "There were close to four thousand entries, and I was one of twenty selected. . . . I was featured on the cover of *USA Today*, and my youngest sister, my mother, and

75

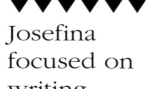

Josefina
focused on
writing
quality roles
for Latinas,
roles that
were more
represen-
tative of the
Latinas she
knew.

JOSEFINA LÓPEZ

I went to Washington, D.C., to receive the award."

Then something highly unusual happened. "At the awards banquet, just before I was presented with the award, I happened to meet the president of my college [Columbia College in Chicago]," says Josefina. "He just happened to be in Washington, D.C., meeting with a senator, when he heard about me. He asked me if the rumors were true that I had dropped out of his college. I told him that they were and that I had tried to get a scholarship from his school, but to no avail. He told me right there that he would give me a full scholarship for however many years I needed to complete my degree. I was so happy, but I was just a little sad that it took a national award in order for me to get someone's attention so that I could get the financial assistance I needed to stay in school."

Even though she encountered difficulties, Josefina constantly kept her mind open and kept writing, no matter where she lived or was going to school. She graduated with a Bachelor of Arts degree in Film and Screenwriting on May 27, 1993 with honors and a 4.0 grade point average. After graduation, she actively pursued a career as a writer. Each project led to the next; playwriting led to scriptwriting, and then to producing.

What had started her in this direction in the first place was the desire to act. But acting is the arm of her profession in which she is least experienced. Back when Josefina entered Los Angeles County High School for the Arts, she had majored in theater with the intention of becoming an actress. The more she studied theater and Hollywood casting practices, the more she believed that "as a Latina actress I would only get to play maids, prostitutes, and unwed teenage mothers," since those were the dominant roles for Latinas. So she focused on writing quality roles for Latinas, roles that were more representative of the Latinas she knew.

It was inevitable

Josefina with Cheech Marin at the screening of *Cisco Kid* in February 1994

that one day she would return to acting. At the age of 25 she was asked to star in her own play *Real Women Have Curves* as the character of Ana Garcia, based on herself at eighteen. Performing the role with the San Diego Repertory Theatre, which was about her own identity, stirred up deep emotions: "On opening night, after the performance, I was so moved by the standing ovation, I started crying. I thanked the audience for being part of my dream come true."

Josefina stays active in theater as she approaches the end of her first decade as a playwright. One of her latest plays, *Confessions of*

It's inconceivable to her that there are so many Latinos living in Los Angeles, yet Hollywood has turned a blind eye to producing stories about them.

JOSEFINA LÓPEZ

Women From East L.A., was staged at the Fritz Theater in San Diego. *Confessions* started out as a one-woman show in which Josefina was to play all the roles. It has evolved into a multiple-woman show featuring four actresses.

Josefina's first foray into writing for film was as a screenwriter for an adaptation of *Real Women Have Curves* in 1990, and for TV as a staff writer on *Living Single* in 1993, both for Warner Bros. In the fall season of 1993, she worked as a writer, performer, and segment producer for an acclaimed but short-lived comedy sketch show on Fox called *Culture Clash*. In 1994 she served as a writer for HBO/Tropix, working on *The Latino Anthology Series*.

Working inside and outside of the Hollywood community, Josefina believes it is important to expose others to her culture. It's inconceivable to her that there are so many Latinos living in Los Angeles, yet Hollywood has turned a blind eye to producing stories about them.

Josefina can't help being political. It is part of her psyche, since she grew up in a political situation as an undocumented immigrant. But hard data supports her assertion that Latinos continue to be underrepresented on television. According to the National Council of La Raza, a leading advocacy group for U.S. Hispanics, in 1984 the representation of Hispanics on network television was only 1 percent of roles, much less than even the 3 percent of the 1960s, when *I*

JOSEFINA LÓPEZ

Love Lucy had a Hispanic main character, Desi Arnaz. In 1995 the figure rose to only 2 percent.

To be so invisible is very insulting to Josefina, especially since she lives in Hollywood and has to fight against the stereotypes everywhere she goes. "Something like 57 percent of the people in Los Angeles are Latino, and yet [network executives continue to produce] shows like *Beverly Hills 90210* and *Melrose Place*. Oh, occasionally you'll have a Latino, and it's just not reality. When kids who grow up seeing television think that's reality, it really messes up their minds, their thinking."

Still, she remains hopeful that gradually Latinos will become acknowledged as a political and artistic presence. "It's just a matter of time," she asserts. "I mean, we're not going to go away. Especially now, with a lot of people like me becoming citizens, we'll have more political power."

To manage all her projects, in January of 1995 Josefina formed a theater, film, and television production company with writer/producer Jon Mercedes III, called Mercedes/López Productions, Inc. The new company is developing projects for television, including a new family situation comedy with Emmy Award-winning producer/writer Norman Lear. Lear is well known as the producer of the TV shows *All in the Family, Sanford and Son, Maude, The Jeffersons*, and a series featuring Latinos—*A.K.A. Pablo*. Josefina's half-hour sitcom about a Latino family is loosely based on

Josefina's partner, Jon Mercedes III

▼▼▼▼▼

"I've been working with Norman Lear, and I really, really respect him," says Josefina.

▲▲▲▲▲▲

her own family and is tentatively called *The Chavez Family*.

Josefina knows how much television can influence young people because of her own memories about the short-lived show *A.K.A. Pablo*. At sixteen, she caught only a few episodes of *A.K.A. Pablo*, starring comedian Paul Rodriguez as the title character, and was extremely disappointed that it was taken off the air. That planted a seed in her mind of wanting to someday write a successful Latino sitcom that would stay on the air for a long time.

The Chavez Family could possibly be that sitcom. The show was written in February of 1996, and a network may give it the green light for production for 1997. She's keeping her fingers crossed. "I've been working with Norman Lear, and I really, really respect him. And we've been working really hard . . . all of us have given it our all. So we're waiting to see. . . . It would be a sin if 1997 comes and there isn't a Latino show on the air."

In addition to *The Chavez Family*, Mercedes/López has two other projects in development for television. One is a half-hour sketch comedy and variety show called *La Fiesta de HA-HA*, which Josefina co-created for the United Paramount Network (UPN). The other project draws upon her experiences at the high school for the arts. Called *Innercity H.S.T.A.*, it's a one-hour drama for NBC that Josefina describes as "sort of like

Fame meets *Beverly Hills 90210"* with Latino characters.

In 1995 she served as artist-in-residence at California State University, Northridge. During her stint there, the university's theater department produced *Unconquered Spirits,* which she had written in 1992. This magical play is about *La Llorona,* the crying woman of Mexican folklore. *La Llorona* is often called "the ghost woman." She was an Indian woman taken by Hernán Cortés, the conqueror of Mexico. She killed her own children to prevent them from being abducted by Cortés and raised as Spaniards. Mexican mothers use the tale of

Josefina jokes with *La Llorona,* a California State University, Northridge production of *Unconquered Spirits* in May 1995.

La Llorona like a bogeyman story; they warn their children not to run off or *La Llorona* might get them. In addition, as Josefina says, "My mother romanticized the story, telling how the Spaniard and the Indian woman fell in love and they had a child, and this and that. . . . Taking away the romanticism, these two people probably could not have fallen in love. They couldn't have because they weren't equal." To Josefina this is a "children's story that bleeds." She sees *La Llorona* as symbolic of the conquest of Mexico.

One of the biggest challenges of Josefina's life has turned out to be one of the great rewards of her life. It also has been the inspiration for much of her work. That challenge is experienced by many children of immigrants—the tension of balancing two worlds. For Josefina it is a balancing act between the old world of her Mexican heritage and the new world of her life as a Hollywood writer. She draws upon her parents' world whenever she wants to, but she has also learned to accept that her parents can never truly understand her new life.

She explains: "Just recently I was awarded a Silver Goddess Award by the Chicano Federation of San Diego for outstanding artistic achievement and exemplary contributions to the Latino community. I had invited my parents to go to the awards ceremony at Hotel Del Coronado in San Diego. I was going to fly them to San Diego and have them ride with me in the limo that was to pick me up and take me to the hotel. I had everything arranged, and, the day before, my parents told me they didn't want to go.

"I was so hurt because this award was very important to me, and they knew it. I wanted to disown them right then and there. I wanted to

Josefina received the Silver Goddess Award for outstanding artistic achievement and exemplary contributions to the Latino community.

stop talking to them from then on. I went to the awards banquet and I received the award and it was no big deal. . . . My parents didn't want to go to the awards banquet because they didn't feel comfortable being at that kind of black-tie event. They didn't have the right clothes, and they didn't want to be there in case I started talking about them and our 'personal' family life.

"After a few weeks I forgave them and accepted that my parents don't understand the world I live and work in and am now a part of. I know they love me, but they don't necessarily have to be a part of my world. When I was growing up, my parents wanted me to graduate from high school, get married, and have children. That was their world, that is what they knew, it was their tradition. I fought so hard not to be a part of that world. That's not who I am, that's not what I wanted to be."

Josefina's goal as a Chicana playwright and writer is to change the negative representation of Latinos in the theater and in Hollywood by actively developing excellent works in all media. She has given a voice to Latinas in the United States, since almost all of her work has been about the Latina experience.

She gave herself a mission: to fill a gap she found when she compared Latinas with other Americans. "When I was just starting out as a writer, I would go to the library and there would be no plays written by Latinas. Today if a young Latina writer goes to the library she will at least

▼▼▼▼▼
Josefina's goal as a Chicana playwright and writer is to change the negative representation of Latinos in the theater and in Hollywood.
▲▲▲▲▲▲

be able to find my plays and those of a few others who have emerged in the last ten years.

"When I was very young I thought that the reason there were no Latinos on television was because our stories were not important enough to be told. I love writing about the Latino experience and having other Latinos realize that our experiences, our stories, and our contributions to the United States are very important. I enjoy having young people come up to me and thank me for writing about our experiences. They often share with me and confide their painful stories.

"I get to tell stories and make people laugh with my writing. Specifically, as a playwright, I get to see my work being performed on stage and see people's reactions. I love to shock people, make them laugh and think at the same time. I get so much satisfaction from writing that if for some reason I weren't allowed to write anymore, I would rather die."

Josefina and her sisters (from left to right): Rosaura, Josefina, Esther, and Angie

In her 27 years on this earth, Josefina López has accomplished more than many people do in a lifetime. She is the first Latina television writer to have a one-hour drama, a half-hour comedy, and a sketch comedy and variety television show being developed simultaneously for three different networks. She wants to challenge herself in other fields, as a film director and a television producer. She

Josefina and the cast and crew of *Confessions of Women from East L.A.* after the show, April 1995

wants to keep acting—in film, theater, and television, if possible.

Her stubbornness and what her parents termed "craziness" have paid dividends. Her refusal to give up under difficult circumstances means that she has succeeded where others might have meekly accepted their lot and done nothing. Who knows where she'll end up next? One thing is sure: whenever Latinos break through barriers in theater, film and television, Josefina López will be leading the charge.

ALFREDO ESTRADA

Publisher, *Hispanic* Magazine
1959-

"Don't limit yourself. You can be whatever you want to be, but you have to work hard. You can't give up. Keep at it.**"**

Alfredo J. Estrada, as told to Barbara Marvis, March 1996

BIO HIGHLIGHTS

- Born March 23, 1959, in Havana, Cuba; mother: Teresa Estrada; father: Alfred Estrada
- 1964, family moved to the United States where his father's climb up the corporate ladder kept the family moving from city to city throughout Alfredo's childhood years
- 1972, lived in Brazil for a year
- 1976, graduated from Brunswick Prep School in Greenwich, Connecticut
- Enrolled at Harvard; earned A.B. in Latin American Studies in 1980
- 1984, earned Juris Doctor degree from University of Texas
- Worked as a corporate lawyer for Kaye, Scholer, Fierman, Hays, and Handler from 1984 to 1987
- 1987, moved to Washington, D.C., to pursue a career in politics
- In April 1988, launched *Hispanic* magazine
- Currently: married to Mary Batts Estrada; they live in Texas

ALFREDO ESTRADA

Being proud of his Cuban heritage is only one factor that entered into Alfredo Estrada's successful launch of *Hispanic* magazine. His constant desire for new challenges, his love of writing and journalism, and his entrepreneurial spirit are all traits that have helped him build his expanding publishing domain. "We strive to be the voice of the Hispanic community," says Alfredo. "We try to provide interesting, exciting stories that show what it means to be Hispanic in this country."

Alfredo José Estrada was born on March 23, 1959, in Havana, Cuba. He is the oldest child and only son of Alfred (Fred) and Teresa Estrada, who were both born in Cuba. His sister Sophia, four years his junior, was born in 1963, and his sister Anne, six years younger, was born in 1965.

Alfredo's father, Fred, was born in Matanzas, Cuba. He earned a Bachelor of Mechanical Engineering degree from the Georgia Institute of Technology in 1954. He then went to work for Shell Oil Company in Cuba and England, starting as an engineering trainee and working his way up to Director of Economics and Scheduling. In 1959, when Alfredo was born, Fred became the Director of Refining for the Cuban Institute of Petroleum. In 1961, the company transferred him, and after a few-month stay in the United States, the family moved to Spain, where Alfredo spent his preschool years.

In 1964, when Alfredo was five, the family returned to the United States —Fred had taken

"We strive to be the voice of the Hispanic community," says Alfredo.

a job managing several projects for Mobil Oil. In Detroit, Michigan, Alfredo attended first grade. His father's continual climb up the corporate ladder kept the family moving throughout the United States and around the world over the next several decades. Alfredo grew up in towns all over the world. "This was not unique for the times," remarks Alfredo. "During the sixties and seventies, large corporations often transferred their employees and their families to many locations. If you wanted to get ahead, you went along."

Alfredo attended second grade in Armonk, New York. In third grade, his father was transferred to Winter Haven, Florida. When Alfredo was in fourth grade, the family moved to Houston, Texas.

In 1972, when Alfredo was thirteen, Fred went to work as a project leader for C.E. Lummus. The family moved to Brazil for a year, and Alfredo attended Chapel School for eighth grade.

The family returned to the United States the following year, and Alfredo attended high

Alfredo's family (from left to right): his grandmother; his mother, Teresa Estrada; his sisters, Anne and Sophia; his father, Fred Estrada; and Alfredo

▼▼▼▼▼▼

"Wherever
we went, I
was proud
of my
Cuban
heritage."

▲▲▲▲▲▲

school at Fairfield Prep in Fairfield, Connecticut. Before he finished there, the family moved one more time, to Greenwich, Connecticut, when Fred became the president of Beker International. Alfredo graduated from Brunswick Prep School in 1976.

Alfredo did very well in school. He was easily able to transfer his knowledge from one school to another, year after year, and maintain a high scholastic average. He learned English at a young age, and the language was never a barrier. He enjoyed traveling. "It was fun to visit new places and meet new people," says Alfredo. "And wherever we went, I was always proud of my Cuban heritage. I could speak Spanish and English, and most of my classmates could not. I had no trouble adapting from one school to the next. It was a big adventure."

Alfredo went on to enroll at Harvard in 1976, majoring in Latin American Studies. He earned an A.B. in 1980. His original intention was to pursue some career in politics or business, and he felt that a law degree might put him in the proper arena. So he enrolled at the University of Texas and earned his Juris Doctor degree in 1984. He passed the New York bar examination, and was entered into the Washington, D.C., bar as well. He moved to New York City and went to work for Kaye, Scholer, Fierman, Hays, and Handler from 1984 until 1987. He was a corporate lawyer specializing in litigation and banking law, but he was also very interested in immigration law and legislative matters relating to Latin America. He represented clients in political asylum cases and worked pro bono (for free) for several public service groups such as Legal Aid.

But corporate law didn't turn out to be exactly what Alfredo wanted. In 1987, he moved to Washington, D.C., thinking he needed a change in his career. At first he thought he might pursue politics, and his move to Washington would bring him closer to this ideal. He went to work helping to raise money for presidential hopeful Michael Dukakis. But in the back of his mind, Alfredo wanted to go into business for himself. He had been very interested in writing and journalism while he was in college, and he thought about this as a career. He was interested in business, he possessed an entrepreneurial spirit, he loved big challenges, and he wanted to do something for the Hispanic community. His own magazine was the answer. In 1987, Alfredo began to make plans for the launch of *Hispanic* magazine.

"As far as positive coverage of Hispanics in the news, it did not exist in mainstream America," says Alfredo. "News about Hispanics, positive or negative, was difficult to find in every major city. What little coverage there was was about crime or violence or drugs. I wanted a magazine that focused on the positive contributions being made by the Hispanic community."

▼▼▼▼▼
Corporate law didn't turn out to be exactly what Alfredo wanted.
▲▲▲▲▲▲

ALFREDO ESTRADA

▼▼▼▼▼▼

The first issue of *Hispanic* was published in April 1988 with a very small staff.

▲▲▲▲▲▲

Alfredo approached his father about his idea. By now, Fred Estrada had founded Pan American Enterprises, a partnership dedicated to venture development and management services. Then he became an investor in, and chairman and CEO of Horizon Communications Company, the publishers of *Vista* magazine. *Vista* is the largest Hispanic publication in the United States, with a monthly circulation of over 1.2 million copies. The magazine is delivered as an insert in newspapers, the same way *Parade* magazine, for example, is circulated. With this experience, Alfredo and his father jointly founded Hispanic Publishing Corporation and made plans to publish *Hispanic* magazine. Fred Estrada became the chairman and CEO of Hispanic Publishing Corporation, and Alfredo assumed the day-to-day operations as publisher and editor of *Hispanic* magazine.

The first issue of *Hispanic* was published in April 1988 with a very small staff. Originally, Alfredo planned the publication to be a Hispanic version of *People Weekly*. The first issues emphasized celebrity and lifestyle features with such stars as actor Edward James Olmos and singer Julio Iglesias on the covers. About two-thirds of the editorial content was about major celebrities. The readers weren't very interested. Neither were the advertisers. "The response was underwhelming," says Alfredo. "It wasn't necessarily what people were interested in. The retail advertisers didn't pay any attention to us. Soon we had to

ALFREDO ESTRADA

pour a lot more money into the company to keep it going."

Alfredo decided to revamp the entire magazine in an effort to attract more readers and advertisers. Instead of reporting on celebrities, *Hispanic* changed its focus to business, government, careers, and education. Celebrity and lifestyle features became about one-quarter of the content. The new mix paid off. Ad pages and circulation increased. By the end of its third year, *Hispanic* was making a profit.

Although Alfredo is bilingual, he knows that many second- and third-generation Hispanics are not. *Hispanic* is published in English to reach the growing population of Hispanics whose first language is English, but who identify strongly with their Latino heritage. *Hispanic* magazine focuses on the American experience, whereas many Spanish-language publications in the U.S. tend to come from Spanish-speaking countries or to feature events and issues outside the United States.

Stories that are covered in *Hispanic* now include up-and-coming role models in politics, business, and education. Features often explore issues of importance to the Hispanic community such as "What Clinton Will Do for Hispanics"; the HISPANIC 100, which annually lists the one hundred companies providing the most opportunities for Hispanics; the Hispanic Achievement Awards, an annual salute to outstanding role models in the Hispanic community; and articles

Alfredo's magazine, *Hispanic*

Alfredo at work

▼▼▼▼▼

Alfredo credits his success to hard work, vision, and determination.

▲▲▲▲▲▲

such as, "G.I. José," which explore what World War II meant to the Hispanics who served. As publisher and editor, Alfredo determines the content of each issue in conjunction with three editors who manage freelance writers and contributors and who research and write many articles themselves.

Alfredo credits his eventual success to hard work, vision, and determination. "One of the toughest obstacles we had to overcome early on was the lack of a broad Hispanic talent pool. We had a difficult time finding Hispanics who had experience in the publishing industry. That forced us to grow our own talent."

Alfredo originally started *Hispanic* in Washington, D.C., but he moved his publication to Austin, Texas, in 1994. "Texas and California are the heart of Hispanic America, and we felt that Austin was a good place to go," remarks Alfredo. "One-third of our subscribers lived in Texas. We also like the lifestyle here. It is relaxed and easygoing, but also dynamic." He and his wife, Mary Batts Estrada, now live in Texas, where they met when they both attended the University of Texas in the early 1980s. Mary and Alfredo were married on May 14, 1988.

Alfredo enjoys the challenges that his magazine presents to him daily. He would be bored, he says, if he didn't have the opportunity to be creative or to explore the challenges of being an entrepreneur. "There is a lot of responsibility in running your own small business," he says.

ALFREDO ESTRADA

"When things go wrong, you have to deal with them; you can't just give them to someone else to fix. There are a lot of joys in running a business. There are good times and bad. You have to learn to deal with both."

Alfredo has big plans for Hispanic Publishing Company. In March 1996, the Estradas published their first issue of *Moderna*, a magazine for women. It will be available quarterly. In April 1996, he launched *Hispanic* OnLine, their new home page on the World Wide Web. It features articles from current and back issues of *Hispanic*, on-line chats, and interviews directed toward the Hispanic population.

Alfredo and his wife, Mary Batts Estrada

"The Hispanic community is really growing and making strides across the board in ways that were very difficult to imagine a few years ago," Alfredo says. "I think Hispanics are really having a tremendous impact on this country, and, hopefully, *Hispanic* magazine is part of that."

Given the increasing respect and continued success of *Hispanic*, it is easy to see how Alfredo Estrada will affect the positive image of Latinos worldwide.

Index